No one could be better qualified than Stuart Morris to gather together the 160 photographs in *Portland Camera*. He was born in 1942 of a Portland family with roots on the Island going back many generations. For many years he has been heavily involved in Environmental and Engineering matters in the area. For 12 years he also represented Portland on the Dorset County Council, until 1985 when he stood down from local politics to write *Portland, An Illustrated History*, the acclaimed first full history of the Island. His interest in Portland's history was fostered by the discovery of ancestral involvement with quarrying, the Breakwater, fishing and even smuggling.

Frontispiece
Portland from the air in the 1970's

PORTLAND CAMERA

STUART MORRIS

THE DOVECOTE PRESS

2. Viewed from Abbotsbury Hill, Chesil Beach sweeps toward the distant peninsula of Portland.

First published in 1990 by the Dovecote Press Ltd
Stanbridge, Wimborne, Dorset BH21 4JD

Designed by the Dovecote Press Ltd
Photoset by The Typesetting Bureau Ltd, Wimborne, Dorset
Origination by Chroma Graphics (Overseas) Pte Ltd, Singapore
Printed by Kim Hup Lee Printing Co Pte Ltd, Singapore

British Library Catalogue in Publication Data
Morris, Stuart
Portland camera
1. Dorset. Portland. Social life, history
1. Title
942.335

ISBN 0-946159-79-3

Contents

Introduction
Acknowledgements
An Island Overview 4-6
Around the Coast 7-21
Chiswell 22-42
Fortuneswell 43-58
Tophill 59-78
Island of Stone 79-100
Transport and Industry 101-115
Portland Harbour 116-127
Island Defences 128-139
People and Parades 140-160

Introduction

Why does Portland hold such a unique fascination to so many? Unlike many conventional places with a single thread of history, the Island's past has so many important themes, each with a rich story.

From the time of the earliest known Portlanders 7000 years ago (of whom there is proven evidence), the Island has been subject to change and development under the combined influences of Man and Nature. The Romans were here in force, and Saxons transformed the landscape to a field pattern still visible today. Portland was one of the first places in Britain to be raided by the Vikings, and the Island was held and defended for the King after the Norman Conquest.

There were nine ancient hamlets or villages on the Island: Southwell, Weston, Wakeham, Easton and Reforne on 'Tophill'; and Chiswell, Maidenwell, Mallams and Fortune's Well at 'Underhill'. Castletown was developed in the late 18th century, and The Grove grew as a community in mid Victorian times.

So what has shaped the Island and its people? Few places of its size have experienced so many momentous events: French raids in mediaeval times; repeated actions in the English Civil war; battles of the Spanish Armada; conflicts with piracy and smuggling; the supply of stone for some of the nation's finest ever buildings including St Paul's Cathedral; the Portland lighthouses of the early 18th century did not prevent countless shipwreck disasters. The photographs show some of the features which played roles through those times.

The impact of the construction of one of the world's greatest harbours and the monumental Victorian defence works can be seen in the events and places featured in many of the photographs. More recently Portland saw part of the Battle of Britain being fought in its skies, and provided for the embarkation of half a million troops on D-Day.

All the more remarkable then that Portlanders' homely customs and unique ancient traditions have held fast even into the 'hi-tech' late twentieth century (in which the island also plays a role), when in other less eventful places such customs disappeared long ago. This is partly due to the almost unique continuance of the historic Court Leet, and being a Royal Manor the Island's proud links with the Crown for centuries have been as close as any in the country, with never any lords or squires to intervene.

When the earliest photographs in this book were taken the entire north and east parts of the Island

3. This 1930's view from Priory shows the changes brought by the early 20th century. A train is passing the 1907 fuel tanks, and another (right) is approaching Portland Station from the Easton line. The gas works dates from 1865, and the school (centre) was built in 1913.

were seething with the activity of convicts, contractors and engineers working on the vast government schemes. However, a visitor arriving on the top of the Island would have seen spread before him fields of grass, corn and other crops – with only the sea beyond – separated by miles of dry stone walls and strip linchets. Wide rough roads led to the scattered villages, and swathes of common grazing land wrapped around the undercliff 'Weares', Verne Hill, The Bill and the settlements. Until the late 19th century the numerous stone quarries were confined to the cliff sides, including the sharp edge of the escarpment above Fortuneswell between West Cliff and Verne Yeates. Only in the 20th century has quarrying seriously eaten into the great field system on Tophill's plateau.

Of an eventful thousand years only the last 130 have been recorded by the camera, but what a tumultuous time that has been. It is through the efforts of the early pioneer photographers, trudging over the Island with heavy wooden cameras, stands, hoods and glass plates, that we can see what they saw. The succeeding century of rapid change and upheaval has been captured by professional and amateur cameras alike, the quality of prints they achieved often exceeding those of modern mass technology. I have included some which are not as clear, or are faded, but which are nevertheless of particular interest.

The large number of 'turn of the century' photographs available to us is partly due to the craze in the 15 years up to the First World War (before telephones) when everyone sent each other picture postcards. Among the early professional photographers of Portland were; J S Coombe, Edgar Cox, H Cumming, Francis Frith, Official photographers of the Royal Engineers, F W George, George Harvey, S J Herbert, C & S Kestin, Frederick King, John Pouncy, Edwin Seward, and W Thompson. I have included photographs of all periods to date, to illustrate the dynamic character of what by any definition is a unique and fascinating place.

STUART MORRIS
Portland

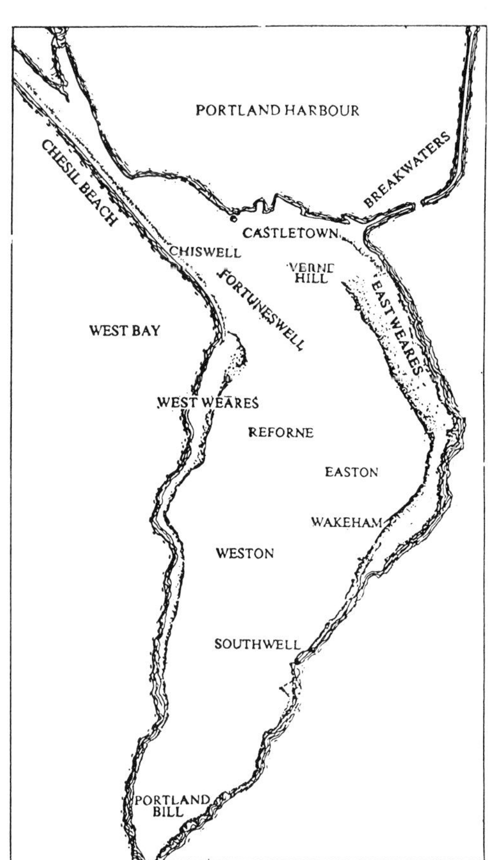

Acknowledgements

I am grateful for the help many people have given me in compiling this work. My particular thanks go to all those who offered me photographs which I was not able to use only through lack of space, and to those who over the years have generously helped me build my personal collection.

I wish to acknowledge the following sources: Edward Andrews; 129, 133, 135, 138, 154. David Burnett; 15, 68. F. Coombes; 110, 111. Dorset County Library (Weymouth Reference Section); 8, 22, 64, 118. Dorset Natural History & Archaeological Society, Dorset County Museum; Front cover, 41, 57. 'Skylark' Durston; 75, 82, 112. Doris Gardner; 28, 29. Monica Gill; 43, 51, 120, 147. W. Hounsell; 130. Andy Hutchings; 119, 145. B. Howarth-Loomes; 80. Ken Lynham; 67, 76, 81, 84, 85, 98, 109. Brian McKinnan; 32. Geoff Moore; 100. HMS Osprey; 1, 7, 78, 117. Richard Phillips; 56. Douglas Smith; 73, 113, 114. Ron Smith (FPN); 31, 59, 81, 143, 144, 149. Royal Corps of Engineers; 91, 131. Irene Sherratt; 115, 137. Greg Stone; 105, 136, 142, 157, 158. Reg Vincent; 2, 21, 35, 36, 52, 159, 160. Weymouth & Portland Museums; 58, 107. Bob Wollage; 150, 156. All the other photographs are from the Author's Collection.

Island Overview

4. *(Above)* This 1967 view looking south shows the impact of quarrying (centre) on the Island landscape. Until the late 19th century virtually all the quarries were on the cliff edges, and the Tophill plateau was mainly pastoral. The settlements of Fortuneswell and Chiswell are lower right and the ramparts of the former Verne Citadel, left.

5. *(Opposite top)* For more than 120 years photographers have recorded the subtly changing scene from Priory on Portland Heights. It is a superb vantage point for Chesil Beach, extending beyond Abbotsbury far away on the mainland. Below is the then still pastoral setting of Underhill in this 1890's view. More than 50 fishing boats are on the beach.

6. *(Opposite below)* Nineteenth century development on this steep hillside joined the old hamlets of Chiswell and Maidenwell (left), Mallams (centre) and Fortuneswell (right). The stone posts and walls are of ancient origin.

Around the Coast

7. An aerial view of Portland Bill from the West showing the Old Higher (left) and Lower (right) Lighthouses. The masts are for long range radio communications. The tranquil fields on the Island contrast with the turbulent sea below West Cliffs.

8. Provisions being delivered to the old Higher Lighthouse around the turn of the century. The first light was erected here in 1716, and this tower dates from 1869.

9. The old Lower Lighthouse shortly before it was de-commissioned in 1906. Later used as a private residence, then a cafe, it was then converted into a Bird Observatory and Field centre, opened by the naturalist Sir Peter Scott in 1961.

10. The tower of the 'new' Lighthouse being erected in 1905. Its beams were first thrown out to the horizon on 11th January 1906.

11. The Portland Bill Lighthouse overlooks the Pulpit Rock (right). Above the cliffs, where quarrymen toiled a century ago, can be seen the famous Raised Beach, a remarkable legacy of high sea levels after the last ice age. Admiralty buildings now occupy most of the exposed 'beach' area seen here in its previous natural state in 1936.

12. As the Bill Lighthouse became a centre of attraction in the 1930 's new cafes joined the old fishermen's huts. Charabancs and cars were soon to bring tourists by the thousand, and over the next 20 years locals filled the mid distance fields with recreational huts. Centre is the track of an old railway to the cliff edge quarries. This view was taken from the top of the lighthouse.

13. *(Above)* Church Ope Cove in about 1895. A delightful setting, but a scene of great activity in the past, not only with fishing but loading of stone barges from long vanished piers, and intense smuggling in the 18th and early 19th centuries. The area is now purely recreational. The posts and winches were used to haul up the boats.

14. *(Left)* Rufus Castle was built to defend Church Ope Cove against invaders from the sea, around the 15th century. It replaced old Saxon defences. In the foreground is an archway to the old church of St Andrew, Portland's main meeting place for 500 years until it was finally abandoned in 1756. The remains of the ruined church were further damaged by a Second World War bomb.

15. *(Opposite page)* A view of Rufus Castle 50 years later. St Andrew's Church ruin has been carefully secured by archaeologists, but the seaward arch of the castle (which can be seen here) collapsed in 1989.

16. Folly Pier Waterworks was built on the the East Weares to provide water for the prison and the great 19th century fortification schemes. Its tanks were used as swimming baths for Borstal Boys in the 1930's, and the whole site has now been almost reclaimed by nature.

17. This ancient salt pool was dug out of the clay Weares below the East Cliffs. It filled at high spring tides and when the basin dried out the salt residue would have been collected from the stone slab sides. Its origin and date are unknown.

18, 19. The dramatic picture below shows the *Madeleine Tristan* laden with grain from France, being driven ashore in Chesil Cove in the morning of 20th September 1930. *(Bottom):* the *Madeleine Tristan* ended up high on the beach to be gradually stripped by storm and salvage over several years. "Dead Mans Bay" off Chesil Beach was one of the most dangerous parts of the British coast in days of sail.

20. *(Above)* Portland rocket crew prepare to rescue survivors from the *Okahandja,* stranded on the rocks below West Cliff in 1910. More than 400 shipwrecks have been recorded in Portland waters since the 17th century.

21. *(Left)* With rotor blades perilously close to Blacknor Cliff, a potholer is rescued by a helicopter from Portland's Royal Naval Air Station, in 1975.

Chiswell

22. Houses in the old fishing village of Chiswell nestle on the leeward slope of Chesil Beach. Passages or 'Opes' lead up from the main street to give rapid access to the beach and sea. Amongst the boats here in 1895 can be seen white linen laid out to bleach in the sun.

23. In the early 1890 's children pose for the photographer outside their picturesque thatched and stone-roofed cottages in Brandy Row. This ancient street had seen centuries of fish trading, sea heroism and plunder of shipwrecks, and of course smuggling, relieving the day to day business of a busy community.

24. Within a few years all these attractive Tudor houses leading to the beach had gone or been reduced to fishing stores. The one still intact here in about 1904 was used by the Coast Watchers in the 1914-18 war.

25. Like most old houses in the area these simple but robust stone cottages facing Chiswell Square had survived countless storms and sea floods. However they did not survive the council's Closure Orders and were demolished in the 1930 's.

26. The sheltered alleyways of old Chiswell gave intimacy to the fishermen's cottages. The 19th century Wesleyan Chapel (right) was later a garage for 50 years, and was cleverly converted to a residence in 1988.

27. A large stone water cistern was erected in Chiswell Square to supply water piped from a spring in West Weares to the village in the 19th century. Unfortunately it was often contaminated and villagers then preferred to go to wells further up the hillside. The tank had a gas lamp on top and a post box in the side. It was demolished in the 1920 's.

28. Keeping the stony main street of Chiswell clean was hard work in 1895. The gables of the 1865 railway station can be seen at the far end of the village.

29. Three Chiswell ladies in their striking late Victorian dresses stand by a whitewashed porch near Clements Lane.

30. A morning sun shines over the roof tops of south Chiswell in 1928. The street had several little Victorian shop fronts, and stone steps and neat dormer windows (left) give character to the old village. The crane at Priory Corner is visible on the skyline.

31. Among the dozen little children (with the staff of this sweet shop by Cove Cottages) are three babies in the cart! The building was converted into flats in the 1920 's and totally restored in a conservation scheme in 1990.

32 *(Above)* A panorama of Victoria Square. The Royal Victoria Hotel (centre) was built by Captain Augustus Manning of Portland Castle for the visitors arriving by the new railway connection in 1865.

33. *(Below)* Part of Chiswell Village (right) from the beach. The old Police House (upper left) at Castle Road lies between Verne Hill's Great and Little Commons. The houses of Queens Row (later 'Road') are centre.

34. Chesil Cove is a favourite bathing spot, capturing the afternoon and evening sun. (Little flesh is exposed by these 1920 's bathing costumes!). Children still have names for each of the big waters' edge rocks.

35. The Cove was 'boiling' with sprats in 1963 when Mervin and Pat Burden, George Boatswain and Jock McGrandle wrestle in the surf to land no less than 8 tons of fish!

36. Chesil Beach, Portland's – and Weymouth's – great natural defence, is under siege in this 1976 storm. As has always occurred every five years or so, the Beach Road was flooded cutting off the Island's communication with the mainland. The beach profile changes and is imperceptibly migrating eastward, but it has never been breached.

37. Chiswell villagers had generations of experience for coping well with the sea floods which were always a feature of life here. The landlady of the Lord Clyde Inn opened the flood ducts under the floor, and apart from losing beer in the cellar, carried on as usual. The Lord Clyde (named after a visiting 19th warship) finally succumbed to Hitler's bombing and was demolished after the war.

38. The 1960 Ford Consul just gets through where its ancestor faltered on the roadside. Over the wall the railway (1865) then the fuel tanks (1907) dammed the natural outlet for the floodwater to The Mere. At peak floods the water easily reached the top of the wall (which was originally built to stop horses shying from steam trains). The problem was only solved when the entire road was raised by 1.5 metres in 1988.

39. Councillor and local builder 'Hoppy' Davies inspects the first stage of the Sea Wall in 1959, the site of the diminishing clay bank. There are actually two walls joined by concrete beams and stone fill over which the promenade was formed.

40. Huge waves washed over Chesil Beach in the greatest sea storms of modern times, in December 1978 and February 1979. This prompted a final major scheme to secure the old village against floods, once and for all.

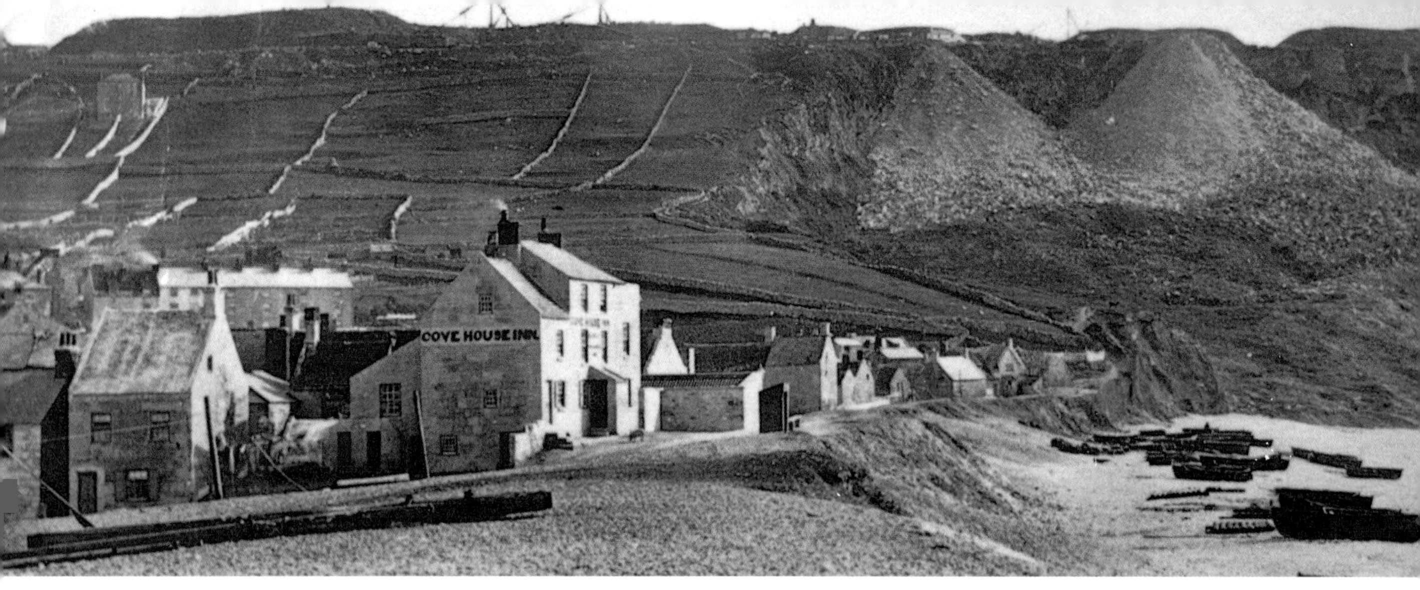

41. The Cove House Inn has stood sentinel over the beach and the village for two hundred years. Spilling down the cliffs is white overburden tipped from the quarry railways (see photograph 80). Fields extend right down to the village here in 1890, but most have now been built on.

42. The old inn suffered unprecedented damage in a storm of December 1989, despite the protection it never had before. However the basic structure remained sound and the popular pub reopened three months later. The original Promenade (1958-1965) withstood the storms well but was reinforced in the 1980 's, giving a new lease of life to the old village as well as being a popular amenity.

Fortuneswell

43. Two lads – perhaps contemplating what the future twentieth century might hold for them – on a stone wall by the Merchants' Railway overlooking Fortuneswell in 1897. The original 1792 Brackenbury Chapel is just beyond the trees (right).

44. A modern view of the top of Fortuneswell. The 'new' Brackenbury Church was completed in 1900. Behind (right) is Brackenbury School, being replaced in 1990 after a 40 year campaign! The three dormer windows are on architect/quarry merchant Thomas Gilbert's "Queen Anne House" of about 1760; the cubic Portland Council Offices were opened in 1934, and the houses (right) were completed in 1989.

45. The former Rectory (upper left) commands a superb view from the top of Old Hill road. The alien architecture of the PUDC Offices stands out, (but at least it is clad in Portland Stone). The tall chimney is on the Portland Steam Laundry, founded in 1900. The still undeveloped fields of Lancridge are beyond in this 1937 photograph.

46. *(Left)* Ancient stone posts and handrail still help on the incredibly steep Old Hill.

48. *(Following page)* These Fortuneswell children stand casually – and safely – across the street to have their photograph taken. Four generations later a pelican crossing was needed to help people cross between ten thousand vehicles passing this spot each day.

47. *(Below)* The fine original Portland Rectory was built at Old Hill soon after St George's Church in the late 18th Century, supported by a high retaining wall on the steep hillside. The Merchants' Railway is just visible in the foreground, and re-appears around the distant Verne Hill, upper right.

49. Crowds witness the foundation stone ceremony for the new Brackenbury Wesleyan Church, Fortuneswell in 1898. Local builder John J. Patten & Sons had the contract, and many prominent Portlanders sponsored the engraved stones. The Church was opened exactly two years later.

50. The tall Victorian shops on the left blocked the sea view of the older Royal Portland Arms (centre right) – until the former were demolished after being bombed in the Second World War. Way's shop (centre) is at the junction with High Street.

51. The houses in High Street (left) were erected on gardens known as Modery Mead in the 1890 's.

52. Snow brings rare tranquillity to Fortuneswell as here in 1978. The building (left), seen as Way's shop in photograph 50, dates from the 18th century.

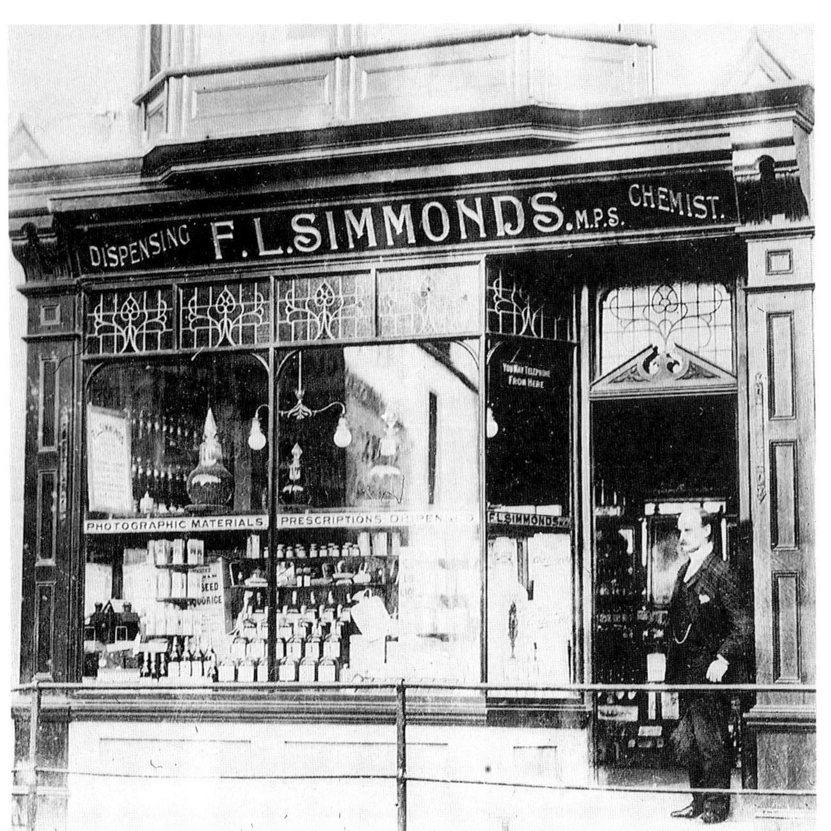

53. *(Left)* Mr Simmonds stands proudly outside his exquisite chemist shop around 1910. Underneath it a spring ran from Verne Hill to emerge as the ancient Fortunes' Well which was just in front of the railing.

54. *(Below)* The bunting is out for big celebrations – possibly the coronation of King Edward VII in 1901. These magnificent Victorian buildings arose after 1863 with new wealth brought to Fortuneswell by the great Breakwater and Verne projects.

55. Traditional street trading continued well into the twentieth century. St John's Church was built on a steep hillside in 1838-40 by John Hancock of Weymouth. Its early Vicars were colourful – and controversial characters.

56. The west side of Verne Hill, where Portlanders had always exercised their common rights, and enjoyed unbounded freedom over buttercup, violet and cowslip fields. Many Roman stone coffins were discovered during work on this large council estate seen here starting in 1950. The houses were prefabricated in a temporary factory near Weston. Portland Police Station (below) was built in 1905. The tower held an early radar antenna.

57. Meissner's Knap, Fortuneswell was named after the Island's first resident surgeon who lived in this part of Fortuneswell. Seen here in 1893 the Royal Hotel (right built by Captain Abraham Scriven in 1863) hosted many important visitors to the Breakwater works.

58. The old gas lamp had given way to overhead electric ones, and from 1932 the Regal Cinema blotted out the view of the church, but here in 1960 all the other Victorian buildings remain hardly altered. Three years later a one-way traffic system was introduced.

Tophill

59. Late in Queen Victoria's reign many shops were formed in the fronts of old cottages, as this one at Straits.

60. Tophill's main streets radiate from Easton Gardens. The Easton & Church Hope Railway (1901-1965) (left) curves around the station. The large building is All Saint's Church. This aerial view was taken around 1960.

61. Traditional Island cottages nestle with taller Victorian buildings in Easton Street, undisturbed by traffic in 1906. Increased use of traction engines after the First World War churned the roads into mud or dust.

62. *(Above)* Easton Square in 1880. Behind the donkey is the Great Pool, once a proper village pond, but by then rather contaminated. This barren place was beautified when public gardens were laid out here 24 years after this photograph was taken.

63. *(Below)* Children earned useful pennies turning the handle to raise water from Easton's well, before a piped supply was laid in 1901. The shaft was dug deep into the bedrock in 1775.

64. *(Following page)* In the warm summer evening after the opening of the gardens in 1904 Easton Square was '.. transformed into a palace of light and movement. A thousand fairy lights glimmered from among the shrubs; children rolled on the lawns while their elders laughed and joked'.

65. *(Left)* A year after they completed the new lighthouse, contractors Wakeham Brothers erected this elegant clock tower in Easton Gardens. Mason Hibbs and Bower worked the stone, and its designer, R. Stevenson Henshaw (centre) displayed another talent when he sang a solo after the unveiling ceremony in May 1907.

66. *(Below)* The freshly completed Easton Gardens, clock, and Wesleyan Chapel were even more a picture after a snow storm in April 1908. The bandstand survived until 1966.

67. *(Above)* Wakeham – an ancient hamlet in its own right - as elsewhere on Tophill has an incredibly wide street. Originally a simple track through common greens, the grass became eroded away as stone traffic increased.

68. St George's Church has dominated the skyline above Easton since 1766. It replaced the old St Andrew's at Church Ope Cove, and has been redundant since 1917. Its superb Georgian architecture has now been lovingly restored.

69. Shepherd Bowring's cottage at Wakeham was burnt down in 1929. Some of the ill-equipped fire brigade arrived by taxi, while children helped mobilise the hand-pump. Every Portland village once had many cottages of this style, but now only two survive intact on the Island.

70. Pennsylvania Castle was the marine mansion of John Penn, grandson of the founder of Pennsylvania USA. Designed by James Wyatt it was completed in 1800. Penn spent the last thirty years of his life enhancing the grounds of his beautiful cliff top estate, overlooking Church Ope Cove.

71. 72. Two views of Portland Museum which was created in two old cottages in 1930. The lower of the pair was built by Bartholemew Mitchell in 1640, and was immortalised as Avice's Cottage by Thomas Hardy in his novel *The Well Beloved.*

73. The gates of Pennsylvania Castle were normally locked to all but distinguished visitors – of which there were many in Victorian times. In 1950 the residence was converted into the fine Pennsylvania Castle Hotel.

74. Each of the Tophill villages became established around natural watering places. For hundreds of years Weston's pond was the scene of women washing, horses drinking and children playing. In 1906 it was filled in after Portland's piped water supply was laid.

75. Little Emily Durston peeps at the photographer from the doorway of her mother's drapery shop at Weston. Her father Harry, the village carpenter and coffin-maker is standing (right) in his workshop above.

76. Southwell, Dorset's most southerly village, is one of Portland's oldest settlements. There is ample evidence of Roman occupation, and nearby Barrow Hill took its name from long-lost pre-historic earth mounds there. To the right of the lamp post is the little Methodist Chapel built in 1849.

77. *(Right)* This neat church on a knoll overlooking Southwell is a memorial to 106 men, women and children who drowned when the clipper *Avalanche* collided with the *Forest* in the Channel south of here in 1877.

78. *(Below)* Until the 1960's Southwell remained a rural village. Its old farm is lower centre, and fishing boats were launched from Freshwater Bay just below the cliffs (right). Portland Bill Road is to the right. As the 20th century progressed a large housing estate was laid out to its West, while the ancient fields of Lime Croft, Suckthumb and Coombe Field separating the village from Weston, were progressively quarried away (top).

Island of Stone

79. The percussive ring of cranked hand cranes was once heard around the hundreds of small Island quarries. Until the mid 19th century all quarrying was driven in from the cliff edges.

80. This rare photograph shows quarrymen in top hats near Priory in about 1870. The rail wagon was used to tip overburden onto the Weares below. In the distance are gardens where Sea View Terrace, Ventnor Road, Albion Crescent and other 19th century housing developments were yet to be built.

81. Steam power was first brought to Portland for the Breakwater works, and by 1890 quarry hand derricks as here were being converted to the new system.

82. Quarry owner A.G.Coombe proudly oversees the cutting of the first turf at Silklake, one of the expanse of fields near Broad Croft, east of Wakeham. The date is 6th June 1910, and over the next 80 years virtually all the farm land on the east of the Island was removed to rebuild some of London's greatest streets.

83. By the 1930's steel cranes were working along with traditional wooden ones, powered by DC electricity.

84. A typical quarry gang invariably included a dog or two – and a daily flagon of ale. The stone was traditionally squared up (using *kivels* and *twybels)* before being moved from the quarry.

85. After squaring, the stone was measured. The marks used to be carved using an old system of strokes, as seen (painted) on the lower stone in contrast to the modern figures, showing the number of cubic feet.

86. This little 2 foot gauge Bagnal steam engine *Excelsior* was brought to Portland by F. J. Barnes and Co. in 1898. It conveyed overburden to the cliffs.

87. The Portland (or Merchants') Railway was constructed in 1826 to take stone from Priory Corner to the loading pier at Castletown. Stone blocks were brought here from the quarries to be loaded by a fixed stub-rooted crane onto four-wheeled flatbed trucks.

88. The original crane at Priory was struck by a thunderbolt in 1927, and was replaced by the one shown here.

PORTLAND STONE

89. A team of heavy horses refuelling from nose-bags before taking the next load on the long journey around the steep hillsides. The track had a gentle and constant gradient.

90. For the first 80 years of the Merchants' Railway stone was brought to Priory by horse-drawn wagons. By 1920 horses had given way to steam traction engines on the roads, but they still hauled the trucks on this railway until it closed in 1939.

91. *(Above)* This remarkable view of 1877 shows the line of the Merchants' Railway (centre) enveloped by the massive formation works of the Verne Citadel. Convicts are filling the deep grassy valley of Tilley Coombe (where 60 years later houses were built) to an even slope to form a defensible 'glacis'.

92. *(Left)* The rails of the Merchants' Railway were removed in 1959 but the track – with stone 'chairs' (sleepers)- remains intact as a public footpath. Above is the large earth pyramid formed in the 1880's to protect the great South Gate of Verne CItadel.

93. Four late 19th century bridges above Tillycoombe. These were built to carry roads over inclines connecting quarries at King Barrow to the Merchants' Railway.

94. At the top of the Merchants' Incline the trucks were unhitched from the horses, and hooked to the end of a steel cable (originally a chain). The cable passed around a brake drum and over wheels down the incline. The other end was hooked to empty trucks, so that gravity was the only motive force needed.

95. The Castletown end of the Merchants' Incline, where horses again took over for the final leg of the journey. The low running costs ensured that the railway made good profits throughout its 112 year existence.

96. The Stone Pier was built for the shipping of stone to London and other southern ports. The Castletown waterfront was much more sheltered than the rest of Portland's coast, even before the Breakwater was constructed.

97. Not all stone was exported via the Merchants' Railway. After 1886 some was taken by traction engines through Fortuneswell to F. J. Barnes' saw mill at Victoria Square. This load is passing the now mature Victoria Gardens around 1924.

98. A fleet of 7.7 litre AEC Mammoth Majors revolutionised the transport of Portland Stone to all parts of the country in the late 1930's. Seen here in 1957, some of the pre-war trucks carried on to chalk up a quarter-century's continuous service. The Bath & Portland Stone Firms' distinctive royal blue livery set off the creamy white cargoes of valuable carved or cut stone.

99. The quality of the work produced by these banker masons in the Wide Street works in the 1920's was matched by their fine singing. Portland's large masonry yards became established after 1870; previously stone had been worked in the quarry or on site.

100. A world famous tradition continues. Geoff Smith and his craftsmen of the Easton Masonry Company produced the entire carved stone facade of the Sainsbury extension to the National Gallery in 1989/90. (Photograph by Geoff Moore).

Transport and Industry

101. "The opening of the few miles of railway alongside the Chesil Bank will bring greater changes than have been wrought throughout Great Britain by anything of like length". So exclaimed *The Illustrated Times* when the line came to Portland in 1865.

102. *(Above)* In laying the Easton and Church Hope Railway up the wild East Weares towards the cliffs the contractors encountered almost impossible ground conditions, as in 1898 when 40,000 tons of cliff fell in the path of the track. This landslip occurred in 1907.

103. *(Above)* The original station terminus at Victoria Square was converted to a goods depot after the line was extended to Easton in 1902. The neat stone building was demolished to make room for a roundabout in 1969.

104. *(Below)* Easton Station was set in a shallow cutting, a delightfully sheltered setting at the end of a truly scenic journey. The railway closed to passengers in 1952, and to goods in 1965. On this site is now Ladymead Hall, an elderly persons home.

105. The branch line to Easton was finally opened in 1902 after 18 years' construction. Climbing steadily around the Island's precipitous east coast, the line plunged through this shear cliff face above Church Ope Cove. Yeolands Bridge was built to carry the public cliff-top path.

106. Farming has been an important Island industry since before recorded time. Being a Royal Manor part of the produce traditionally went to the King or Queen. These horses are working a field at Portland Bill in 1921. (The Higher Light is on the hilltop, left).

107. Ploughing 'Out by Windmills'. Portland's two mills are probably 400 years old, and last turned in the 1890's.

108. For centuries Portland Sheep were famous for their delicacy, and the mutton graced many a royal table. They grazed on the commons around the cliffs and over Verne Hill. They were washed before shearing in the Mere, near Chiswell. Once almost extinct the rare breed is again thriving on the Island.

109. The staff and workers of Crown Farm, the ancient Demesne farm owned by the royal Lord of the Manor. The buildings at Grove Corner, Easton were bombed in 1942 and finally demolished in 1977.

110. The turn of the century saw a transformation in the quality of life on the Island. A piped water supply enabled enterprises like the Portland Steam Laundry to be started. Here the laundry's driver Sam Coombes waters his horse at Easton Lane. Behind are the old Crown Farm buildings.

111. Steam Laundry Proprietor Richard Score and his staff outside the original (1879) Masonic Hall in Victoria Square.

112. The smart Members of the new Portland Urban District Council pose for posterity on a quarry railway in 1896. This body replaced the inefficient – even corrupt – old Local Board the previous year. It was dissolved in 1974.

113. *"Room for more?"* Children from St John's, Fortuneswell pile into Smith's wagonette for a ride to the Grove.

114. The first car managed to reach Tophill in 1904, but motor transport flourished after the First War. Here is cab proprietor R. J. Smith at Wakeham with his soft covered motor brake the body of which was converted from a horse-drawn wagon.

115. Portland Fire Brigade, formed in 1901, enjoyed only 2 years of independence after commissioning their spanking new fire engine in 1938. They were absorbed into the National Fire Service in 1940.

Portland Harbour

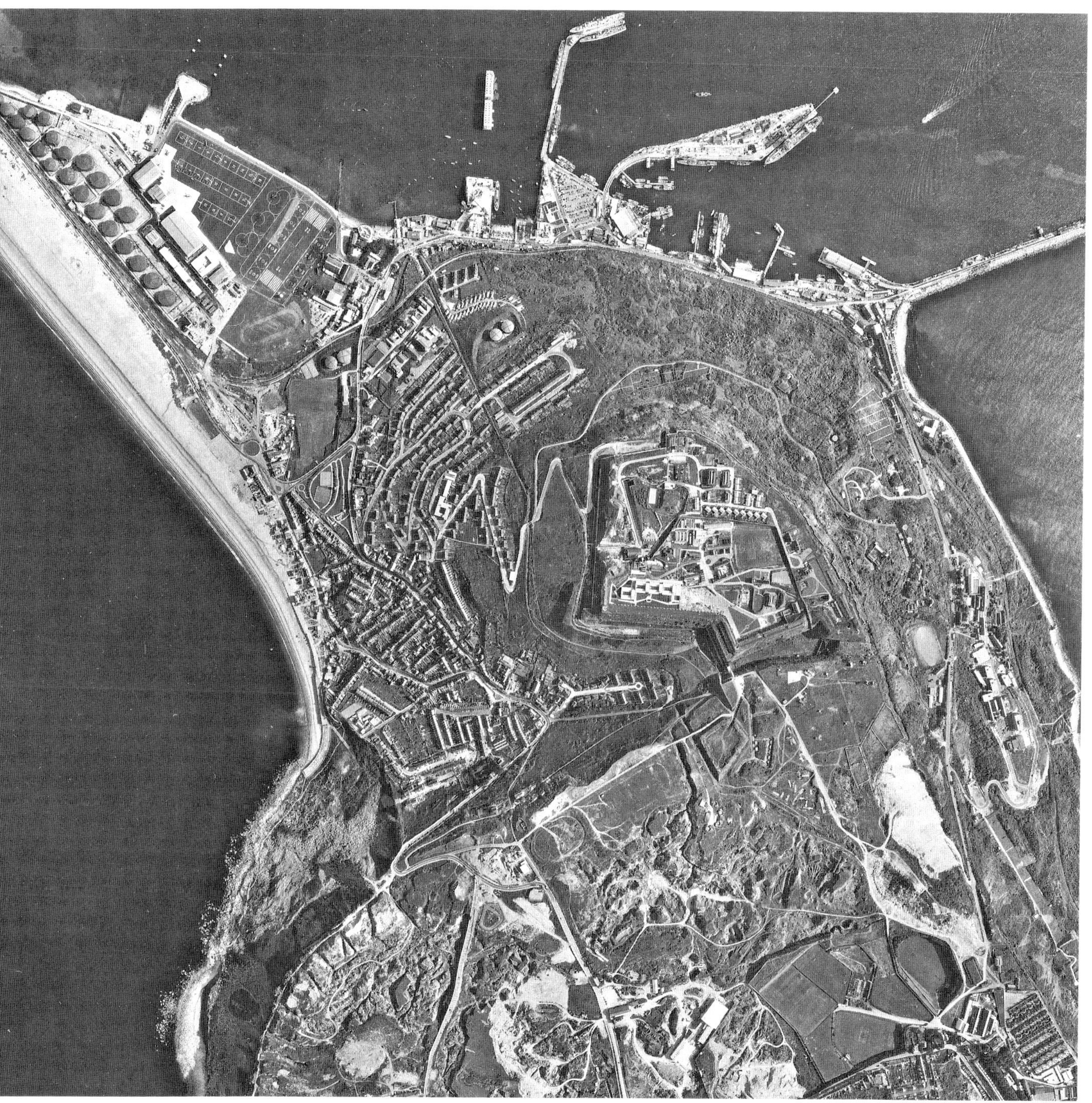

116. Fortuneswell and The Verne (centre), Castletown (top), part of the Breakwater and East Weares (right), and the intricate 19th century quarry cuttings, (bottom). Behind Chesil Beach is the RN Air station on land reclaimed from the tidal Mere. This photograph was taken in 1972.

117. An aerial view of the Dockyard and part of the RN Air Station in the 1960s.

118. Castletown (seen here in 1890) developed with the growth of trade and the Navy from the late 18th century. By the 1850's it was the hub of stupendous activity for the Portland Breakwater works, and shops, services and hotels soon followed. Fishing here suffered as the long beach was squeezed by a century of naval development.

119. The bay windows of Castletown's single Victorian terrace enjoyed a panoramic view over the beach to Portland Harbour. The old Post Office is seen here (centre) in about 1898.

120. Portland Castle was built for Henry VIII in about 1530, and saw much action during the Great Civil War between 1642 and 1646. This well preserved Ancient Monument is regularly open to the public.

121. Sheltered by the new Breakwaters, the waterfront of Portland Harbour was rapidly developed. With the arrival of steam vessels a huge coaling pier was started in 1891. The ship seen here was Portland's training ship HMS *Boscowen.*

122. The Coaling Pier as first built was an expensive failure – ships could not birth close enough to the tipped stone sides! By the time it was rebuilt in 1905 coal-powered ships were becoming obsolete and the first of the oil fuel tanks were being erected.

123. The tide entered the large natural wetland of The Mere via The Gut, a narrow channel through Coneygar Bank. By 1906 the relentless Admiralty development reached here also. Shingle from nearby Chesil Beach was tipped as base fill for the enormous fuel tank 'farm'. Thus ended a unique wildfowl habitat.

124. Both the railway embankment (left) and the fuel tank farm – here under construction in 1907 – blocked the natural outlet of floodwater from Chiswell, with dire consequences. The mile long pipe (right) carried sand for filling which steam pumps sucked from the bed of Portland Harbour; more than 50 men are working in this scene. Chesil Beach is on the far left.

125. *(Above)* After the Second War there was plenty of room in Portland Harbour for the Royal Navy's greatest ever warships, the aircraft carriers. Eight *Phoenix* units (part of the wartime Mulberry Harbour which was floated to Dunkirk) were brought here in 1946 to shelter new pier construction.

126. *(Below)* The Greek steamer *Patroclus* was one of the few to escape after striking the rocks under West Cliff, in 1907. She was towed into Portland Harbour to be pumped out and repaired, only to be lost in the Great War. The warships behind exemplify the great naval arms race with Germany which was then starting.

127. *(Below)* Flying pioneers graced Portland skies from the earliest years of powered flight. Here Cdr. Sansom prepares to fly out to greet King George V in 1912. Unfortunately the plane ditched into the sea and had to be towed back.

Island Defences

128. The first convicts came to Portland in 1848 to produce stone for the Breakwater works. The Convict Quarries near the Grove were the model of orderliness, and discipline was strict. By late Victorian time tourists were coming by the thousand to see them at work.

129. The original convict cells at Grove Prison were lined with iron. The Prison was rebuilt at the end of the last century, and was converted into a Borstal Establishment in 1921.

130. Alma Terrace at The Grove displays bold architecture of the 1860's. The taller of these Prison staff houses seen here were demolished in 1989. The Grove is now a Conservation Area.

131. Temporary railway lines were laid for cutting the cavernous ditch around the top of Verne Hill. The construction the Verne Citadel and Portland's other defences was the largest single government project of the time. This is the building of the South Caponier in 1865. The work took more than twenty years to complete.

132. The South Gate and Caponier today. The Verne Citadel (now a Scheduled Monument) was taken over by the Prison Department in 1948.

133. *(Above)* Officers of the 2nd Somerset Light Infantry relax on the steps by the main square of Verne Citadel, prior to embarking to the Boer War in November 1899.

134. *(Left)* Military parades and band concerts brought vibrant colour and music to Islanders. This 1st Somerset Regiment was stationed at the Verne from 1908 to 1911 and is seen here marching from the South Gate.

135. The power of a steam traction engine was harnessed through its winch to haul a gun up Meissner' Knap, Fortuneswell.

136. A slight loss of ceremonial dignity as a little girl crawls through the legs of officers of the Portland 'Terriers' in 1933. For the third time they had won the coveted King's Cup shooting competition.

137. As with all Portland's heavy armaments, getting this 9.2inch gun up to Blacknor Fort on West Cliff in 1909 was a major operation.

138. *(Above)* Preparing to fire a gun at the High Angle Battery, over East Cliff, in 1899.

139. *(Below)* Portland's intense activities in the Second World War came to a climax with the embarkation of half a million US troops on D-Day. here amphibious 'DUKWS' stand by on specially hardened ground on the causeway near the harbour. This later became the recreational Chesil Beach car park.

People and Parades

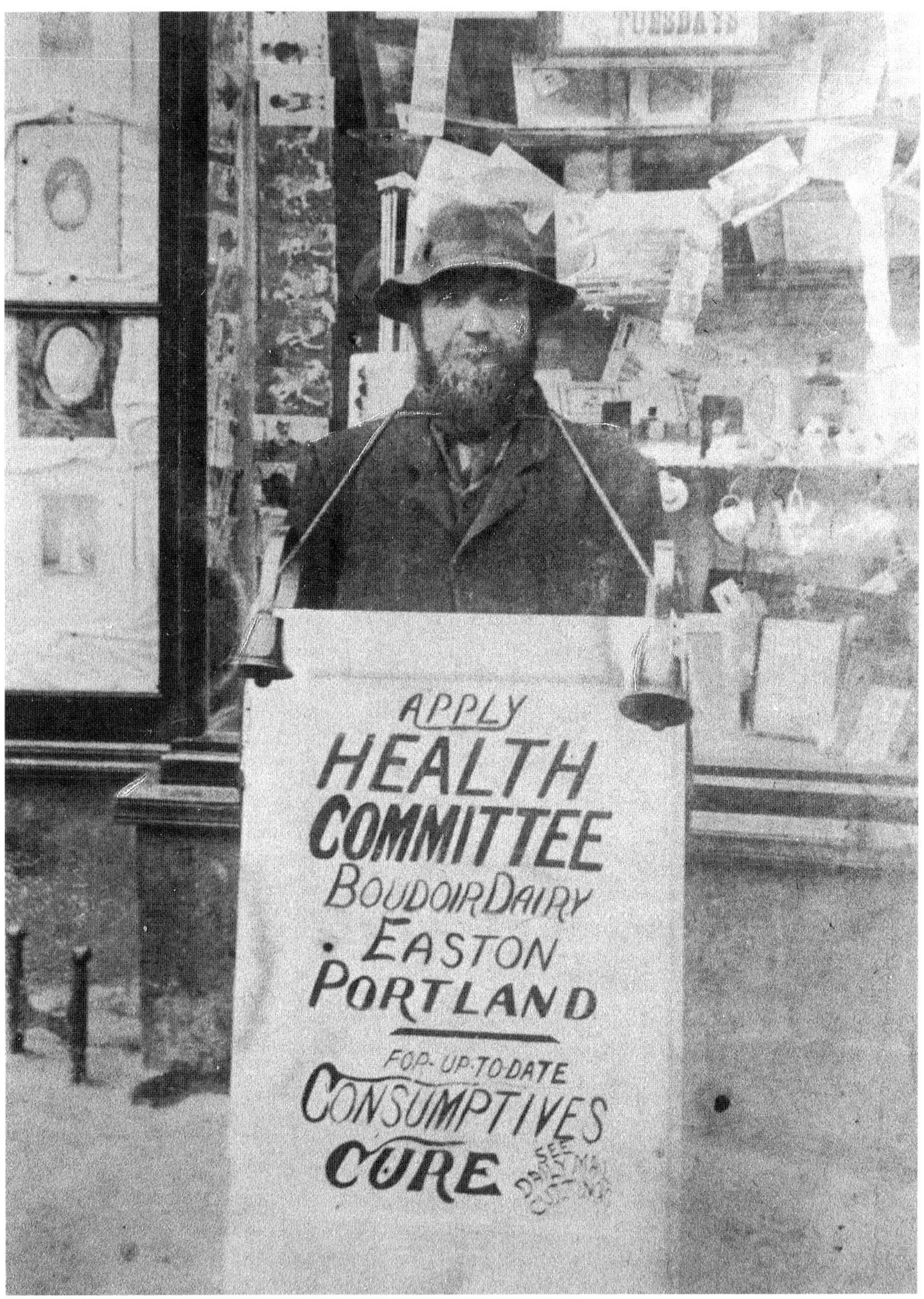

140. Whether the cure for 'consumption' (tuberculosis) offered by Billy the board man was effective is not known!

141. The historic Court Leet has protected the rights and privileges of the Royal Manor of Portland for probably a thousand years. It is virtually unique in still having legal powers. Here the Court of 1900 stands outside the George Inn, Reforne. The Reeve is holding the staff on which was marked the payments made in each of the Island's villages.

142. The handsome carriage and pair (c1908) belonging to Henry 'Gaffer' Sansom, quarry owner, of Pennsylvania Castle.

143, 144. Daily deliveries of bakers', butchers' and dairy produce were made around the Island.

145. A man doffs his hat as a funeral cortege passes the *Prince of Wales Inn,* Fortuneswell. (It was the Prince of wales who laid the last stone of the original Breakwater, in 1872).

146. Wakeham was packed in March 1908 for the untimely funeral of popular Richard Lano, Captain of the Portland Volunteer Artillery, who died after serving in the African Boer War. Note the old thatched cottage on the right, one of many to be demolished between the wars.

147. A Naval band leads a long procession of sailor cadets – in white dress and best 'sennet' hats – through Fortuneswell, watched by Edwardian Portlanders.

148. *(Below)* Portland Men's Own Brotherhood organised several successful carnivals, before and after the First World War. This procession is about to climb New Road to Tophill in about 1906.

149. *(Following page)* From the 1880's countless processions of all descriptions passed through Fortuneswell. This is tail end of a carnival procession in about 1925.

COMBEN

150. Apart from their uniform laced boots, these Victorian Easton school children sport an assortment of dress styles! In their lifetime the Island changed, in parts beyond recognition. Fortunately many of their 'adventure playgrounds' – the beaches, Weares and old quarries – remain for future generations to enjoy.

151. Banners held aloft for Children's Day 1899 on Little Common, five years before the Victoria Gardens were laid out.

152. Underhill Children parade up Queens Road carrying a large silken banner of the Fortuneswell and Chiswell Sunday Schools, around 1906.

153. Cosens' paddle steamer *SS Premier* lands passengers at Church Ope Cove for a tea-party in the grounds of Pennsylvania Castle. The event in July 1911 was to raise funds to build the new All Saint's Church.

154. The Portland Cycle Club had their first annual meeting at the Clifton, The Grove, in 1893. The solitary penny-farthing must have found the Island's steep roads hard going.

155. Mugs, whistles, lanyards and drums are the order of the day for these early Boy Scouts and Cubs on parade by the side of the Lord Clyde Inn, Chiswell. These buildings were badly damaged by German bombing.

156. Preparing for Weston Village Fete 1922. Many elders still frowned at 'decadent' jazz!

157. A stagecoach races along West Cliff! Portland's bright, clear air has attracted many big film-makers, this exiting shot being for *Midshipman Easy* starring Margaret Lockwood and Hughie Green in 1936.

158. An open-air museum was the project for Class 4st of Tophill Junior School in 1979. Portland's rich natural surroundings are ideal for Environmental Studies led by enthusiastic teachers such as Greg Stone (rear left). Retired farmer the late Jack Comben of Crow Farm (hatted) brought the recent past to life for these children.

159. A cacophony of car horns echoed across Portland Heights when crowds watched the Queens Silver Jubilee Bonfire lit on Verne Yeates in 1977. Not far from the ancient signal beacon site the fire was one of a coastal chain, started by the Queen at Windsor.

160. 900 years of Portland's recorded history were celebrated through the summer of 1978. A climax was the unveiling of the *Tower Stone* in Victoria Square by the Governor of the Tower of London – the earliest national building known to have used Portland Stone.